Charles Nordhoff

America for free working men!

Charles Nordhoff

America for free working men!

ISBN/EAN: 9783337283292

Printed in Europe, USA, Canada, Australia, Japan

Cover: Foto ©ninafisch / pixelio.de

More available books at **www.hansebooks.com**

16. Other current loans, discounts and advances to the public ...
17. Notes and bills discounted overdue and not specially secured.
18. Other overdue debts not specially secured ....
19. Notes and bills discounted overdue and other overdue debts secured by mortgage or other deed on real estate, or by deposit of or lien on stock, or by other securities ....
20. Real estate, the property of the Bank (other than the Bank premises) ....
21. Mortgages on real estate sold by the Bank...... ....
22. Bank premises................... ....
23. Other assets not included under the foregoing heads.............

$ _____

Aggregate amount of loans to and liabilities, direct or indirect, of Directors, and firms or partnerships in which they or any of them have any interest, $

Average amount of specie held during the month, $

Average amount of Dominion Notes held during the month, $

How attested. I declare that the above Return has been prepared under my directions and is correct according to the books of the Bank.

E. F.,
Chief Accountant.

We declare that the foregoing Return is made up from the books of the Bank, and that to the best of our knowledge and belief it is correct, and shews truly and clearly the financial position of the Bank ; and we further declare that the Bank has never at any time during the period to which the said Return relates, held less than forty per cent. of its cash reserves in Dominion Notes.

(*Place*)   this   day of

A. B., *President.*
C. D., *General Manager.*

Special returns may be called for, In addition to the Returns specified in this section, the Minister of Finance shall also have power to call for special Returns from any particular Bank, whenever, in his judg-

William Wilson

An Act Relating to Banks and Banking
The act thirty-fourth Victoria, chapter five

ISBN/EAN: 9783337120924

Printed in Europe, USA, Canada, Australia, Japan

Cover: Foto ©Suzi / pixelio.de

More available books at **www.hansebooks.com**

BANKS AND BANKING.

The Act thirty-fourth Victoria, chapter five, intituled :
"An Act relating to Banks and Banking," with the
amendments made by subsequent Acts* incorporated
with it so as to form one Act.

WHEREAS, it is desirable that the provisions relating to **Preamble.**
the Incorporation of Banks, and the laws relating to
Banking, should be embraced, as far as practicable, in one
general Act ; Therefore Her Majesty, by and with the advice
and consent of the Senate and House of Commons of Canada.
enacts as follows :—

1. The Charters or Acts of Incorporation of the several **Charters con-**
Banks enumerated in the Schedule B to this Act (including **tinue 1 to 1st July, 1881.**
any amendments thereof now in force) are continued as to
their Incorporation, the amount of Capital Stock, the amount
of each share of such stock, and the chief place of business
of each respectively, until the first day of July in the year
of our Lord one thousand eight hundred and eighty-one,
subject to the right of any such Bank to increase its Capital
Stock in the manner hereinafter provided ; and as to other
particulars this Act shall form and be the. Charters of the
said Banks respectively, until the first day of July, 1881, and
the provisions thereof shall apply to each of them respectively, and their present Charters shall be repealed, except
only as to the matters for which the said Charters are above
continued until the day last aforesaid ; and

2. The said Charters or Acts of Incorporation of the several **And to 1st**
Banks mentioned in the Schedule B to this Act, to all **July, 1891.**
which this Act applies, are hereby continued and shall remain in force, subject to the provisions of this Act, until the
first day of July, in the year of our Lord one thousand eight
hundred and ninety-one, except in so far as they or any of
them may be or become forfeited or void under the terms
thereof or of this Act or any other Act passed or to be
passed in that behalf, by non-performance of the conditions
of such Charters respectively, insolvency or otherwise. 34
V., c. 5, s. 1, *and* 43 V., c 22, s. 11.

2. The provisions of this Act shall apply to any Bank to **To what**
be hereafter incorporated (which expression in this Act in- **banks the Act applies.**

---

* 35 V., c. 8 ; 36 V., c. 43 ; 38 V., c. 17 ; 40 V., c. 44 ; 42 V., e. 45, and 43 V.,
c. 22

1

cludes any Bank incorporated by any Act passed in the present Session or in any future Session of the Parliament of Canada), whether this Act is specially mentioned in its Act of Incorporation or not, as well as to all Banks and their branches in any part of Canada (except where otherwise expressly mentioned) whose Charters are hereby continued, but not to any other, unless extended to it under the special provisions hereinafter made. 34 V., c. 5, s. 2.

Matters to be provided for in special Act. **3.** The capital stock of any new Bank, the amount of each share, the name of the Bank, and the place where its chief office shall be situate, shall be declared in the Act of Incorporation of any Bank to be hereafter incorporated. 34 V., c. 5, s. 3.

GENERAL REGULATIONS.

Branches and agencies. **4.** The Bank may open branches or agencies and offices of discount and deposit and transact business at any place or places in the Dominion. 34 V., c. 5, s. 4.

Increase of capital. **5.** The capital stock of the Bank may be increased, from time to time, by the shareholders at any annual general meeting, or any general meeting specially called for that purpose; and such increase may be agreed on by such proportions at a time as the shareholders shall determine, and shall be decided by the majority of the votes of the shareholders present at such meeting in person or represented by proxy. 34 V., c. 5, s. 5.

How to be allotted. **6.** Any of the original unsubscribed capital stock, or the increased stock of a Bank, shall, when the Directors so determine, be allotted to the then shareholders of the Bank *pro rata*, and at such rate as shall be fixed by the Directors, provided always that no fraction of a share shall be so allotted; and any of such allotted stock as shall not be taken up by the shareholder to whom such allotment has been made, within three months from the time when notice of the allotment has been mailed to his address, may be opened for subscription to the public, in such manner and on such terms as the Directors shall prescribe. 34 V., c. 5, s. 6.

Conditions previous to commencing business by new banks. **7.** No Bank to be hereafter incorporated, unless it be otherwise provided by its Charter, shall issue notes or commence the business of Banking until five hundred thousand dollars of Capital have been *bonâ fide* subscribed and one hundred thousand dollars have been *bonâ fide* paid up, nor until it shall have obtained from the Treasury Board a certificate to that effect, which certificate shall be granted by the Treasury Board when it is proved to their satisfaction that such amounts of capital have been *bonâ fide* subscribed and paid respectively; and if at least two hundred thousand dollars of the subscribed Capital of such Bank has not been

paid up before it shall have commenced business, such further amount as shall be required to complete the said sum shall be called in and paid up within two years thereafter, and it shall not be necessary that more than two hundred thousand dollars of the stock of any Bank, whether incorporated before or after the passing of this Act, be paid up within any limited period from the date of its incorporation. 34 V., c. 5, s. 7.

8. The amount of notes intended for circulation, issued by the Bank and outstanding at any time, shall never exceed the amount of its unimpaired paid up Capital : No such note for a less sum than four dollars shall be issued or re-issued by the Bank, and all notes for a less sum heretofore issued shall be called in and cancelled as soon as may be practicable.   34 V., c. 5, s. 8 ; *but see s.* 78 *as to notes issued after* 1st *July*, 1881.   *Amount and denomination of bank notes.*

9 The Bank shall always receive in payment its own notes at par at any of its offices and whether they be made payable there or not ; but shall not be bound to redeem them in specie or Dominion notes at any place other than where they are made payable : the place or one of the places at which the notes of the Bank shall be made payable shall always be its chief seat of business.   34 V., c. 5, s. 9 ; *and see s.* 78 *after* 1st *July*, 1881, *as to proportion of payment in Dominion Notes.*   *Redemption of notes.*

10. No dividend or bonus shall ever be made so as to impair the paid up Capital, and if any dividend or bonus be so made, the Directors knowingly and wilfully concurring therein, shall be jointly and severally liable for the amount thereof, as a debt due by them to the Bank ; and if any part of the paid up Capital be lost, the Directors shall, if all the subscribed stock be not paid up, forthwith make calls upon the Shareholders to an amount equivalent to such loss ; and such loss (and the calls, if any) shall be mentioned in the Return then next made by the Bank to the Government ; provided that in any case where the Capital has been impaired as aforesaid, all net profits shall be applied to make good such loss.   34 V., c. 5, s. 10.   *Dividend not to impair capital. Capital lost to be made up.*

11. No division of profits, either by way of dividends or bonus, or both combined, or in any other way, exceeding the rate of eight per cent. per annum, shall be paid by the Bank, unless, after paying the same, it shall have a rest or reserved fund equal to at least twenty per cent. of its paid up Capital, deducting all bad and doubtful debts before calculating the amount of such rest.   34 V., c. 5, s. 11.   *Dividend limited unless there is a certain reserve.*

12. Certified lists of the Shareholders, (or of the principal partners, if the Bank be *en commandite*,) with their additions and residences, and the number of shares they respectively   *Lists of shareholders to be laid before Parliament.*

1½

hold, shall be laid before Parliament every year, withi fifteen days after the opening of the Session. 34 V., c. ! s. 12.

Monthly returns to Government. **13.** Monthly returns shall be made by the Bank to th Government in the following form, * and shall be made u within the first ten days of each month, and shall exhibi the condition of the Bank on the last juridical day of th month preceding ; and such monthly returns shall be signe by the Chief Accountant, and by the President, or Vice President, or the Director (or, if the Bank be *en commandit* the principal partner) then acting as President, and b the Manager, Cashier, or other principal officer of the Ban at its chief seat of business :—

Return of the Liabilities and Assets of the on the   day of   A.D. 18

Capital authorized.....................$
Capital subscribed.....................$
Capital paid up..........................$

LIABILITIES.

1. Notes in circulation............... $
2. Dominion Government deposits payable on demand..............
3. Dominion Government deposits payable after notice or on a fixed day.........................
4. Deposits held as security for the execution of Dominion Government contracts and for Insurance Companies..............
5. Provincial Government deposits payable on demand..............
6. Provincial Government deposits payable after notice or on a fixed day........................
7. Other deposits payable on demand.........................
8. Other deposits payable after notice or on a fixed day............
9. Loans from or deposits made by other Banks in Canada secured.........................
10. Loans from or deposits made by other Banks in Canada unsecured ....
11. Due to other Banks in Canada...

---

* This form applies to returns made on or after the 1st July, 1880. Until tha date the form hitherto used is in force.

12. Due to Agencies of the Bank or to other Banks or Agencies in foreign countries.............. ......

13. Due to Agencies of the Bank, or to other Banks or Agencies in the United Kingdom............

14. Liabilities not included under foregoing heads................

$ _____

ASSETS.

1. Specie ....$

2. Dominion Notes ....

3. Notes of and checks on other Banks......... ....

4. Balances due from other Banks in Canada ....

5. Balances due from Agencies of the Bank or from other Banks or Agencies in foreign countries.

6. Balances due from Agencies of the Bank or from other Banks or Agencies in the United Kingdom ....

7. Dominion Government debentures or stock ....

8. Provincial, British or Foreign or Colonial public securities other than Canadian.............

9. Loans to the Government of the Dominion ....

10. Loans to Provincial Governments

11. Loans, discounts or advances for which stock, bonds or debentures of municipal or other Corporations, or Dominion, Provincial, British or Foreign or Colonial public securities other than Canadian, are held as collateral securities...........

12. Loans, discounts or advances on current account to Municipal Corporations ....

13. Loans, discounts or advances on current account, to other Corporations ....

14. Loans to or deposits made in other Banks secured ....

15. Loans to or deposits made in other Banks unsecured.........

William Wilson

An Act Relating to Banks and Banking

The act thirty-fourth Victoria, chapter five

ment, the same are necessary in order to a full and complete knowledge of its condition. 34 V., c. 5, s. 13, *as amended by* 43 V., c. 22, s. 4.

14. The Bank shall always hold, as nearly as may be practicable, one-half of its cash reserves in Dominion Notes, and the proportion of such reserves held in Dominion Notes shall never be less than forty per cent. thereof. 34 V., c. 5, s. 14, *as amended by* 43 V., c. 22, s. 3. Part of reserve to be in Dominion notes.

15. Every Bank to which this Act applies shall be exempt from the tax now imposed on the average amount of its notes in circulation, to which other Banks will continue liable, and from the obligation to hold any portion of its capital in Government Debentures or Debentures of any kind. 34 V., c. 5, s. 15. Exemption from bank tax.

16. The Receiver General shall make arrangements as may be necessary for ensuring the delivery of Dominion Notes to any Bank, in exchange for an equivalent amount of specie, at the several offices at which Dominion Notes will be redeemable, in the cities of Toronto, Montreal, Halifax, and St. John (N.B), respectively. 34 V., c. 5, s. 16 ; *and see as to other cities 43 V., c. 13, s. 4 on page* 39. Supply of Dominion notes.

INTERNAL REGULATIONS.

Shares and Shareholders.

17. Books of subscription may be opened, and shares of the capital stock of the Bank may be made transferable, and the dividends accruing thereon may be made payable, in the United Kingdom of Great Britain and Ireland, in like manner as such shares and dividends are respectively made transferable and payable at the head office of the Bank ; and to that end the Directors may from time to time determine the proportion of the shares which shall be so transferable in the United Kingdom, and make such rules and regulations, and prescribe such forms, and appoint such agent or agents, as they may deem necessary. 34 V., c. 5, s. 17. Subscription and transfer of stock in United Kingdom.

18. The shares of the capital stock shall be paid in by such instalments, and at such times and places as the Directors shall appoint, and executors, administrators and curators paying the instalments upon the shares of deceased shareholders shall be and are respectively indemnified for paying the same : Provided always, that no share or shares shall be held to be lawfully subscribed for, unless a sum equal to at least ten per centum on the amount subscribed for be actually paid at the time or within thirty days af er the time of subscribing. 34 V., c. 5. s. 18. Payment of shares. Proviso.

19. The shares of the capital stock of the Bank shall be held and adjudged to be personal estate, and shall be assignable and transferable at the chief place of business of the Bank or at any of its branches which the Directors shall appoint for that purpose, and according to such form as the Directors shall prescribe ; but no assignment or transfer shall be valid unless it be made and registered and accepted by the party to whom the transfer is made, in a book or books to be kept by the Directors for that purpose, nor until the person or persons making the same shall, if required by the Bank, previously discharge all his, her or their debts or liabilities to the Bank, which may exceed in amount the remaining stock, if any, belonging to such person or persons valued at the then current rate ; and no fractional part or parts of a share, or less than a whole share, shall be assignable or transferable.

When any share of the said capital stock shall have been sold under a writ of execution, the officer by whom the writ shall have been executed shall, within thirty days after the sale, leave with the cashier, manager, or other officer of the Bank, an attested copy of the writ, with the certificate of such officer endorsed thereon, certifying to whom the sale has been made, and thereupon (but not until after all debts and liabilities of the holder or holders of the share to the Bank, and all liens existing in favor of the Bank thereon, shall have been discharged as hereinafter provided), the President, Vice-President, Manager or Cashier of the Bank shall execute the transfer of the share so sold to the purchaser ; and such transfer being duly accepted, shall be, to all intents and purposes, as valid and effectual in law as if it had been executed by the holder or holders of the said share,—any law or usage to the contrary notwithstanding. 42 V., c. 45, s. 1. (*Substituted for* 34 V., c. 5, s. 19.)

20. A list of all transfers of shares registered each day in the books of the Bank, showing the parties to such transfers and the number of shares transferred in each case, shall be made up at the end of each day and kept at the chief office of the Bank for the inspection of its shareholders. 34 V., c. 5, s. 20.

21. If the interest in any share or shares in the capital stock becomes transmitted in consequence of the death or bankruptcy or insolvency of any shareholder, or in consequence of the marriage of a female shareholder, or by any other lawful means than by a transfer according to the provisions of this Act, such transmission shall be authenticated by a declaration in writing, as hereinafter mentioned, or in such other manner as the Directors of the Bank shall require, and every such declaration shall distinctly state the manner in which, and the party to whom, such shares shall have been transmitted, and shall be by such party made and signed ; and every such declaration shall be by the party making and signing the same acknowledged before a Judge of a Court of Record, or before the Mayor, Provost or Chief Magistrate of a city, town, borough, or other place, or before a Public Notary, where the same shall be made and signed ; and every declaration so signed and acknowledged shall be left with the Cashier, Manager or other officer or agent of the Bank, who shall thereupon enter the name of the party entitled under such transmission in the Registry of shareholders ; and until such transmission shall have been so authenticated no party or person claiming by virtue of any such transmission shall be entitled to receive any share of the profits of the Bank, or to vote in respect of any such share or shares : Provided always, that every such declara- Proviso. tion and instrument as by this and the following section of this Act is required to perfect the transmission of a share or shares in the Bank which shall be made in any other country than Canada, or some other of the British colonies in North America, or in the United Kingdom of Great Britain and Ireland, shall be further authenticated by the British Consul or Vice-Consul, or other the accredited representative of the British Government in the country where the declaration shall be made, or shall be made directly before such British Consul or Vice-Consul or other accredited representative : and provided also that nothing in this Act contained shall Proviso. be held to debar the Directors, Cashier or other officer or agent of the Bank from requiring corroborative evidence of any fact or facts alleged in any such declaration. 34 V., c. 5, s. 21.

22. If the transmission of any share of the capital stock Transmission by marriage of female shareholder. be by virtue of the marriage of a female shareholder, the declaration shall be accompanied by a copy of the register of such marriage, or other particulars of the celebration thereof, and shall declare the identity of the wife with the holder of such share, and shall be made and signed by such female shareholder and her husband ; and it shall be competent to them to include therein a declaration to the effect that the share transmitted is the sole property, and under the sole control of the wife, that she may receive and grant receipts for the dividends and profits accruing in respect thereof, and dispose of and transfer the share itself, without requiring the consent or authority of her husband ; and such declaration shall be binding upon the Bank and the parties making the same, until the said parties shall see fit to revoke it by a written notice to that effect to the Bank ; and further, the omission of a statement in any such declaration, that the wife making the same is duly authorized by her husband to make the same, shall not cause the declaration to be deemed either illegal or informal ; any law or usage to the contrary notwithstanding. 34 V., c. 5, s. 22.

Transmission by decease. **23.** If the transmission have taken place by virtue of any testamentary instrument, or by intestacy, the probate of the will, or any letters of administration, or act of curatorship, or an official extract therefrom, shall, together with such declaration, be produced and left with the Cashier, or other officer or agent of the Bank, who shall, thereupon, enter the name of the party entitled under such transmission, in the register of shareholders. 34 V., c. 5, s. 23.

Further provision in such case. **24.** If the transmission of any share or shares of the capital stock of the Bank be by the decease of any shareholder, the production to the Directors and the deposit with them of any authenticated copy of the probate of the will of the deceased shareholder, or of letters of administration of his estate granted by any Court in the Dominion having power to grant such probate or letters of administration, or by any prerogative, diocesan or peculiar Court or authority in England, Wales, Ireland, or any British Colony, or of any testament testamentary or testament dative, expede in Scotland, or, if the deceased shareholder shall have died out of Her Majesty's dominions, the production to and deposit with the Directors of any authenticated copy of the probate of his or her will or letters of administration of his or her property, or other documents of like import granted by any Court or authority having the requisite power in such matters, shall be sufficient justification and authority to the Directors for paying any dividend, or transferring, or authorising the transfer of any share or shares, in pursuance of and in conformity to such probate, letters of administration, or other such document as aforesaid. 34 V., c. 5, s. 24.

Provision in case of doubt as to person entitled. **25.** Whenever the interest in any share or shares of the capital stock of the Bank shall be transmitted by the death of any shareholder or otherwise, or whenever the ownership of or legal right of possession in any such share or shares shall change by any lawful means other than by transfer, according to the provisions of this Act, and the Directors of the Bank shall entertain reasonable doubts as to the legality of any claim to and upon such share or shares of stock, then, and in such case, it shall be lawful for the Bank to make and file in one of the Superior Courts of Law or Equity in the Province in which the Head Office of the Bank is situated, a declaration and petition in writing, addressed to the Justices of the Court, setting forth the facts and the number of shares previously belonging to the party in whose name such shares stand in the books of the Bank, and praying for an order or judgment adjudicating and awarding the said shares to the party or parties legally entitled to the same, and by which order or judgment the Bank shall be guided and held fully harmless and indemnified and released from all and every other claim for the said shares or arising therefrom : Provided always, that notice of such petition shall be

Proviso.

given to the party claiming such share or shares, or to
the Attorney of such party duly authorized for the purpose,
who shall, upon the filing of such petition, establish his
right to the several shares referred to in such petition ; and
the delays to plead and all other proceedings in such cases
shall be the same as those observed in analogous cases before
the said Superior Courts : Provided also, that the costs and Proviso.
expenses of procuring such order and adjudication shall be
paid by the party or parties to whom the said shares shall be
declared lawfully to belong, and such shares shall not be
transferred until such costs and expenses be paid, saving the
recourse of such party against any party contesting his right.
34 V., c. 5, s. 25.

26. The Bank shall not be bound to see to the execution Bank not
of any trust, whether expressed, implied, or constructive, to bound to see
to trusts.
which any of the shares of its stock shall be subject, and the
receipt of the party in whose name any such share shall stand
in the books of the Bank, or, if it stands in the name of more
parties than one, the receipt of one of the parties shall be a
sufficient discharge to the Bank for any dividend or any other
sum of money payable in respect of such share, unless express notice to the contrary has been given to the Bank ; and
the Bank shall not be bound to see to the application of the
money paid upon such receipt, whether given by one of such
parties or all of them.   34 V., c. 5, s. 26.

2. No person holding stock in any Bank as executor, ad- Executors
ministrator, guardian or trustee, of or for any person named and trustees
not person-
in the books of the Bank as being so represented by him or ally liable.
her, shall be personally subject to any liabilities as a stock-
holder, but the estate and funds in his or her hands shall be
liable in like manner and to the same extent as the testator,
intestate, ward or person interested in such trust-funds
would be, if living and competent to hold the stock in his or
her own name ; and if the trust be for a living person, such
person shall also himself or herself be liable as a shareholder ;
but if such testator, intestate, ward or person so represented Exception.
is not so named in the books of the Bank, the executor, ad-
ministrator, guardian or trustee shall be personally liable in
respect of such stock, as if he or she held it in his or her own
name as owner thereof.   43 V., c. 22, s. 2.

27. Each shareholder in the Bank shall, on all occasions on Votes on
which the votes of the shareholders are to be taken, have one shares.
vote for each share held by him for at least thirty days before
the time of meeting.   Shareholders may vote by proxy, but
no person but a shareholder shall be permitted to vote or
act as such proxy ; and no Manager, Cashier, Bank Clerk.
or other subordinate officer of the Bank shall vote either in
person or by proxy, or hold a proxy for that purpose.   All
questions proposed for the consideration of the said share-

holders shall be determined by the majority of their votes ; the Chairman elected to preside at any such meeting of the said shareholders shall vote as a shareholder only, unless there be a tie, in which case (except as to the election of a Director) he shall have a casting vote ; and where two or more persons are joint holders of shares, it shall be lawful that one only of such joint holders be empowered by letter of attorney from the other joint holder or holders, or a majority of them, to represent the said shares, and vote accordingly ; and in all cases when the votes of the shareholders are taken the voting shall be by ballot. 34 V , c. 5, s. 27 ; *and see s. 30a as to payment of calls ; and as to proxies, s. 78, after 1st July, 1881.*

By-laws may be made.

28. The shareholders in the Bank shall have power to regulate by by-law the following matters incident to the management and administration of the affairs of the Bank, viz: the qualification and number of the directors, which shall not be less than five nor more than ten, and the quorum thereof ; the method of filling up vacancies in the Board of Directors whenever the same may occur during each year ; and the time and proceedings for the election of directors, in case of a failure of any election on the day appointed for it :—the remuneration of the President, Vice-President and other directors ; and the closing of the transfer book during a certain time not exceeding fifteen days, before the pay-

Qualification of director.

ment of each semi-annual dividend :—Provided that no director shall hold less than three thousand dollars of the stock of the Bank, when the paid up Capital thereof is one million dollars or less, nor less than four thousand dollars of stock when the paid up Capital thereof is over one million and does not exceed three millions, nor less than five thousand dollars of stock when the paid up Capital thereof exceeds three millions ; the Directors shall be elected annually

Election.

by the shareholders and shall be eligible for re-election ; Provided that the foregoing provisions, touching Directors, shall not apply to a Bank *en commandite*, which shall in these matters be governed by the provisions of its Charter.

Discounts to directors.

The shareholders (or if the Bank be *en commandite*, the principal partners), may also regulate by by-law the amount of discounts or loans which may be made to Directors (or if the Bank be *en commandite* to the principal partners), either jointly or severally, or to any one firm or person, or to any

Certain by-laws continued.

shareholder or to corporations ; Provided that until it is otherwise ordered by by-law under this section, the by-laws of the Bank on any matter which can be regulated by by-law under this section, shall remain in force, except as to any provision fixing the qualification of Directors at an amount less than that hereby prescribed ; and no person shall be a Director unless he possesses the number of shares hereby required or such greater number as may be required by any by-law in that behalf. 34 V , c. 5, s. 28.

13

29. Any number not less than twenty-five of the sharehold- Special general meetings. ers of the Bank who together may be proprietors of at least one-tenth of the paid-up capital stock of the Bank, by them-selves or by their proxies, or the Directors of the Bank, or any four of them, shall have power at any time to call a special general meeting of the shareholders of the Bank, to be held at their usual place of meeting upon giving six weeks' previous public notice, specifying in such notice the • object or objects of such meeting ; and if the object of any such special general meeting be to consider of the proposed removal of the President, or Vice-President, or of a Director or Directors of the said Bank for maladministration or other specified and apparently just cause, then if a majority of the votes of the shareholders of such meeting be given for such removal, a Director or Directors to replace him or them shall be elected or appointed in the manner provided in the by-laws of the Bank, or if there be no by-laws providing there-for, then by the shareholders at such meeting ; and if it be the President or Vice-President who shall be removed, his office shall be filled up by the Directors (in the manner pro-vided in case of a vacancy occurring in the office of President or Vice-President) who shall choose or elect a Director to serve as such President. 34 V., c. 5, s 29. *And see s.* 30*a as to payment of calls.*

President and Directors

30. The stock, property, affairs and concerns of the Bank Board of directors. shall be managed by a Board of Directors, the number to be fixed as herein provided, who shall choose from among them-selves a President and Vice-President ; the Directors shall be natural born or naturalized subjects of Her Majesty, and shall be elected on such day in each year as may be or may have been appointed by the Charter or by any by-law of the Bank, and at such time of the day and at such place where the head office of the Bank is situate, as a majority of Direc-tors for the time being shall appoint ; and public notice shall Notice. be given by the Directors, by publishing the same at least four weeks in a newspaper of the place where the said head office is situate, previous to the time of holding such elec-tion ; and the election shall be held and made by such of the shareholders of the Bank as have paid all calls made by the Directors and as shall attend for the purpose in their own proper persons or by proxy, and all elections for Direc-tors shall be by ballot, and the said proxies shall only be Proxies. capable of being held and voted upon by shareholders then present, and the persons, to the number fixed by by-law, as hereinbefore provided, who have the greatest number of votes at any election, shall be Directors ; provided that if it should happen at any election that two or more persons have an equal number of votes, and the election or non-election of one or more of such persons as a Direc-tor or Directors depends on such equality, then the Directors who shall have had a greater number, or the majority of them, shall determine which of the said persons so having an equal number of votes shall be the Director or Directors, so as to complete the full number ; and in case of a

Vacancies. vacancy occurring in the number of Directors, such vacancy shall be filled in the manner provided by the by-laws, but the non-filling of the vacancy shall not vitiate the acts of a quorum of the remaining Directors ; and if the vacancy so created shall be that of a President or Vice-President, the Directors at the first meeting, after completion of their number, shall, from among themselves, elect a President or Vice-President, who shall continue in office for the remainder of

Election of the year. And the said Directors, as soon as may be after
president, &c. the said election, shall proceed in like manner to elect by ballot two of their number to be President and Vice-President ; Provided always, that no person shall be eligible to be or continue a Director, unless he shall hold, in his name and for his own use, stock in the said Bank to the amount hereinbefore provided. 34 V., c. 5, s. 30. *And see* s. 30a *as to payment of calls.*

Ss. 27, 29 and **30a.** It is the true intent and meaning of sections twenty-
30 explained. seven, twenty-nine and thirty of this Act that no shareholder in any Bank to which those sections apply has any right to vote, either in person or by proxy, on any question proposed for the consideration of the shareholders of such Bank at any meeting of such shareholders, or in any case where the votes of the shareholders of such Bank are taken, without having paid all calls made by the Directors which have then become due and payable. 40 V 44.

Provision in **31.** In case it should happen that an election of Directors
case of failure should not be made on any day when it ought to have been
of election. made, the Corporation shall not for that cause be deemed to be dissolved, but it shall be lawful on any other day to hold and make an election of Directors in such manner as shall have been provided by the by-laws made by the shareholders in that behalf ; and the Directors then in office shall remain so until a new election shall be made. 34 V., c. 5, s. 31.

Quorum, &c. **32.** At all meetings of the Directors of the Bank not less than three of them shall constitute a board or quorum for the transaction of business; and at the said meetings the President, or in his absence, the Vice-President, or in their absence, one of the Directors present to be chosen *pro tempore,* shall preside ; and the President, Vice-President, or President *pro tempore* so presiding, shall vote as a Director, and if there be an equal division on any question shall have a casting vote. 34 V., c. 5, s. 32.

General **33.** The Directors for the time being, or a majority of them,
powers of shall have power to make such by-laws and regulations (not
directors. repugnant to the provisions of this Act or the laws of the Do-

minion of Canada) as to them shall appear needful and proper touching the management and disposition of the stock, property, estate and effects of the Bank, and touching the duties and conduct of the officers, clerks and servants employed therein, and all such other matters as appertain to the business of a Bank, and shall also have power to appoint as many officers, clerks and servants for carrying on the said business, and with such salaries and allowances as to them may seem meet; and they may also appoint a Director or Directors for any branch of the Bank : Provided always, that before per- Proviso. mitting any Cashier, officer, clerk or servant of the Bank to enter upon the duties of his office, the Directors shall require him to give bond or other security to the satisfaction of the Directors, for the due and faithful performance of his duties ; Provided also, that all by-laws of the Bank lawfully made Proviso. before the passing of this Act, as to any matter respecting which the Directors can make by-laws under this section (including any by-laws for establishing a guarantee fund for the employees of the Bank) shall remain in force until they are repealed or altered by others made under this Act. 34 V., c. 5, s. 33.

34. The Directors shall have power to make such calls of Calls, and money from the several shareholders for the time being upon how enforced the shares subscribed for in the Bank by them respectively, by action. as they may find necessary, and in the corporate name of the Bank to sue for, recover and get in all such calls, or to cause and declare such shares to be forfeited to the Bank in case of non-payment of any such call ; and an action may be brought to recover any money due on any such call, and it shall not be necessary to set forth the special matter in the declaration, but it shall be sufficient to allege that the defendant is holder of one share or more, as the case may be, in the capital stock of the Bank, and is indebted to the Bank for a call or calls upon such share or shares, in the sum to which the call or calls amount, as the case may be, stating the amount and number of such calls, whereby an action hath accrued to the Bank to recover the same from such defendant by virtue of this Act ; And it shall be sufficient to maintain such action, to prove by any one witness, (a shareholder being competent) that the defendant, at the time of making any such call, was a shareholder in the number of shares alleged, and to produce the by-law or resolution of the Directors making and prescribing such call, and to prove notice thereof, given in conformity with such by-law or resolution ; and it shall not be Proviso. necessary to prove the appointment of the Directors or any other matter whatsoever; provided that such calls shall be made at intervals of not less than thirty days, and upon notice to be given at least thirty days prior to the day on which such call shall be payable ; and no such call shall exceed ten per cent. of each share subscribed. 34 V., c. 5, s. 34.

Calls, and how enforced by forfeiture.

35. Provided also, that if any shareholder or shareholders refuse or neglect to pay any or either of the instalments upon his, her, or their shares of the said capital stock at the time or times appointed by such call, as aforesaid, such shareholder or shareholders shall incur a forfeiture to the use of the Bank of a sum of money equal to ten per centum on the amount of such shares; and, moreover, it shall be lawful for the Directors of the Bank (without any previous formality other than thirty days' public notice of their intention), to sell at public auction the said shares, or so many of the said shares as shall, after deducting the reasonable expenses of the sale, yield a sum of money sufficient to pay the unpaid instalments due on the remainder of the said shares and the amount of forfeitures incurred upon the whole: and the President or Vice-President, Manager or Cashier, of the Bank shall execute the transfer to the purchaser of the shares of stock so sold; and such transfer being accepted, shall be as valid and effectual in law as if the same had been executed by the original holder or holders of the shares of stock there-

Proviso.

by transferred; Provided always, that nothing in this section contained shall be held to debar the Directors, or the shareholders at a general meeting, from remitting either in whole or in part, and conditionally or unconditionally, any forfeiture incurred by the non–payment of instalments as aforesaid, or to prevent the Bank from enforcing the payment of any call or calls by suit in lieu of declaring the same forfeited. 34 V., c. 5, s. 35.

Statement to be laid before annual meeting.

36. At every annual meeting of the shareholders for the election of Directors, the out-going Directors shall submit a clear and full statement of the affairs of the Bank, containing on the one part the amount of the capital stock paid in, the amount of notes of the Bank in circulation and net profits made, the balances due to other Banks and institutions, and the cash deposited in the Bank, distinguishing deposits bearing interest from those not bearing interest— and on the other part, the amount of the current coin, the gold and silver bullion, and the amount of Dominion Notes in the vaults of the Bank, the balances due to the Bank from other Banks and institutions, the value of the real and other property of the Bank, and the amount of debts owing to the Bank, including and particularizing the amounts so owing upon bills of exchange, discounted notes, mortgages, and other securities,—thus exhibiting on the one hand the liabilities of, or the debts due by the Bank, and on the other hand the assets and resources thereof; and the said statement shall also exhibit the rate and amount of the last dividend declared by the Directors, the amount of reserved profits at the time of declaring the said dividend, and the amount of debts due to the Bank, overdue and not paid, with an estimate of the loss which will probably accrue thereon. 34 V., c. 5, s. 36.

37. The books, correspondence and funds of the Bank shall at all times be subject to the inspection of the Directors ; but no shareholder not being a Director shall be allowed to inspect the account of any person dealing with the Bank. 34 V., c. 5, s. 37. *Inspection of books, &c.*

38. It shall be the duty of the Directors of the Bank to make half-yearly dividends of so much of the profits of the Bank as to the majority of them may seem advisable, and not inconsistent with the provisions of sections ten and eleven of this Act ; and to give public notice of the payment of such dividends at least thirty days previously. 34 V.. c. 5, s. 38 *Dividends.*

POWERS AND OBLIGATIONS OF THE BANK.

Loans, Interest, Advances on Warehouse Receipts, &c.

39. The Bank shall have the power to acquire and hold real and immovable estate for its actual use and occupation, and the management of its business, and to sell or dispose of the same, and other property to acquire in its stead, for the same purposes. 34 V , c. 5, s. 39. *Real estate for occupation.*

40. The Bank shall not, either directly or indirectly, lend money or make advances upon the security, mortgage or hypothecation of any lands or tenements, or of any ships or other vessels, nor upon the security or pledge of any share or shares of the capital stock of the Bank, or of any goods, wares or merchandize, except as authorized in this Act ; nor shall the Bank, either directly or indirectly, deal in the buying and selling or bartering of goods, wares or merchandize, or engage or be engaged in any trade whatever, except as a dealer in gold and silver bullion, bills of exchange, discounting of promissory notes and negotiable securities, and in such trade generally as appertains to the business of Banking ; nor shall the Bank, either directly or indirectly purchase or deal in any share or shares of the capital stock of the Bank, except where it is necessary to realize upon any such share or shares held by the Bank as security for any pre-existing and matured debt. 34 V., c. 5, s. 40, *as amended by* 38 V., c. 17, s. 1. *Business of the bank defined.*

41. The Bank may take, hold and dispose of mortgages and hypotheques upon personal as well as real property, by way of additional security for debts contracted to the Bank in the course of its business ; and the rights, powers and privileges which the Bank is hereby declared to have or to have had in respect of real estate mortgaged to it, shall be held and possessed by it, in respect of any personal estate which may be mortgaged or hypothecated to it. 34 V., c. 5, s. 41. *Mortgages as additional security.*

42. The Bank may purchase any lands or real estate offered for sale under execution or in insolvency or under *Purchase of land under execution, &c.*

2

the order or decree of a Court of Equity as belonging to any debtor to the Bank, or exposed to sale by the Bank under a power of sale given to it for that purpose, in cases where, under similar circumstances, an individual could so purchase, without any restriction as to the value of the lands which it may so purchase, and may acquire a title thereto as any individual purchasing at sheriff's sale or under a power of sale, in like circumstances, could do, and may take, have, hold and dispose of the same at pleasure. 34 V., c. 5, s. 42, *as amended by* 43 V., *c.* 22, *s.* 5.

Absolute title may be acquired.

43 The Bank may acquire and hold an absolute title in or to land mortgaged to it as security for a debt due or owing to it, either by obtaining a release of the equity of redemption in the mortgaged property, or by procuring a foreclosure in any Court of Chancery or of Equity, or by other means whereby, as between individuals, an equity of redemption can by law be barred, and may purchase and acquire any prior mortgage or charge on such land :

Proviso.

Provided always, that no Bank shall hold any real or immovable property howsoever acquired, except such as shall be required for its own use, for any period exceeding seven years from the date of the acquisition thereof. 34 V., c. 5, s. 43, *as amended by* 43 V., c. 22, s. 6.

Power of sale, &c.

44. Nothing in any Charter, Act or law shall be construed as ever having prevented or as preventing the Bank from acquiring and holding an absolute title to and in any such mortgaged lands, whatever the value thereof may be, or from exercising or acting upon any power of sale contained in any mortgage given to it or held by it, authorizing or enabling it to sell or convey away any lands so mortgaged. 34 V., c. 5, s. 44.

As to advance for building ships.

***44a.** Any Bank advancing money in aid of the building of any ship or vessel, shall have the same right of acquiring and holding security upon such ship or vessel while building and when completed, either by way of mortgage, hypothec, hypothecation, privilege or lien thereon, or purchase, or transfer thereof, as individuals have in the province wherein such ship or vessel is being built, and for that purpose shall be authorized to avail itself of all such rights and means of obtaining and enforcing such security, and shall be subject to all such obligations, limitations and conditions, as are by the law of such province conferred or imposed upon individuals making such advances. 35 V., c. 8, s. 7.

Interpretation of various terms.

45. For the purposes of this Act, the words "goods, wares and merchandize," when used herein, shall be held to comprise, in addition to the things usually understood thereby,

---

* This section applies only to the Provinces of Ontario, Quebec, Nova Scotia and New Brunswick.

timber, deals, boards, staves, saw-logs, and other lumber, petroleum, crude oil, and all agricultural produce and other articles of commerce; and the words "warehouse receipt" when used herein shall be held to mean any receipt given by any person, firm or company for any goods, wares or merchandize in his or their actual, visible and continued possession, as bailee or bailees, in good faith, and not as of *But see s. 47 as to case* his or their own property, and shall comprise receipts from *where the* any person who is the keeper of any harbour, cove, pond, *owner is himself a ware-* wharf, yard, warehouse, shed, storehouse, tannery, mill or *houseman, &c.* other place in Canada, for goods, wares or merchandize being in the place or in one or more of the places so kept by him, whether such person is engaged in other business or not, and shall also comprise specifications of timber. The words "bill of lading," when used herein, shall comprise all receipts for goods, wares or merchandize, accompanied by an obligation to transport the same from the place where they were received to some other place, whether by land or water, or partly by land and partly by water, and by any mode of carriage whatever; and the words "ship" or "shipment" shall be held to mean the delivery of any article for transport as aforesaid. 43 V., c. 22, s 7. (*Substituted for* 34 V., c. 5, s. 45.)

46. The Bank may acquire and hold any warehouse receipt or bill of lading as collateral security for the payment of any debt incurred in its favor in the course of its banking business; and the warehouse receipt or bill of lading so acquired shall vest in the Bank, from the date of the acquisition thereof, all the right and title of the previous holder or owner thereof, or of the person from whom such goods, wares and merchandize were received or acquired by the Bank if the warehouse receipt or bill of lading is made directly in favor of the Bank instead of to the previous holder or owner of such goods, wares and merchandize. And if the previous holder of such warehouse receipt or bill of lading be the agent of the owner of the goods, wares and merchandize mentioned therein, within the meaning of the fifty-ninth chapter of the Consolidated Statutes of the late Province of Canada (which is contained in Schedule "A," appended to this Act, and which, as respects such meaning, shall apply to all the Provinces of Canada), then the Bank shall be vested with all the right and title of the owner thereof, subject to his right to have the same re-transferred to him, if the debt as security for which they are held by the Bank, be paid : Provided always, that the Bank shall not *Proviso.* acquire or hold any warehouse receipt or bill of lading to secure the payment of any bill, note or debt, unless such bill, note or debt be negotiated or contracted at the time of the acquisition thereof by the Bank, or upon the understanding that such warehouse receipt or bill of lading would be transferred to the Bank, but such bill, note or debt may

Warehouse receipts may be taken as collateral security.

Exchange of warehouse receipt for bill of lading and *vice versâ*. be renewed or the time for the payment thereof extended, without affecting such security. And on shipment of any goods, wares and merchandize for which a Bank holds a warehouse receipt, it may surrender such receipt and receive a bill of lading in exchange therefor; or on the reception of any goods, wares and merchandize for which it holds a bill of lading, it may surrender such bill of lading, store such goods, wares and merchandize, and take a warehouse receipt therefor; or ship them or part of them, and take another bill of lading therefor. 43 V., c. 22, s. 7. (*Substituted for 34 V., c. 5, s. 46.*)

When warehouseman, &c., is also the owner. **47.** If any person granting a warehouse receipt or bill of lading is engaged in the calling, as his ostensible business, of keeper of a yard, cove, wharf or harbour, or of warehouseman, miller, saw-miller, maltster, manufacturer of timber, wharfinger, master of a vessel, or other carrier by land or by water, or by both, curer or packer of meat, tanner, dealer in wool, or purchaser of agricultural produce, and is at the same time the owner of the goods, wares and merchandize mentioned in such warehouse receipt or bill of lading, any such warehouse receipt or bill of lading, and the right and title of the Bank thereto and to the goods, wares and merchandize mentioned therein, shall be as valid and effectual as if such owner, and the person making such warehouse receipt or bill of lading, were different persons.

Sale of goods on non-payment of debt. 2. In the event of the non-payment at maturity of any debt secured by a warehouse receipt or bill of lading, the Bank may sell the goods, wares and merchandize mentioned therein, or so much thereof as will suffice to pay such debt with interest and costs, returning the overplus, if any, to the person from whom such warehouse receipt or bill of lading, or the goods, wares and merchandize mentioned therein, as the case may be, were acquired; but such power of sale shall be subject to the provisions hereinafter made. 43 V., c. 22, s. 7. (*Substituted for 34 V., c. 5, s. 47.*)

As to goods manufactured from articles pledged. **48.** If any miller, maltster, or packer or curer of pork grants a warehouse receipt for any cereal grains or hogs which may be manufactured into flour or malt, pork, bacon or hams, respectively, while held thereunder, such warehouse receipt shall vest in any Bank which shall be or become the lawful holder thereof, all the right and title to such manufactured article, which such Bank acquired under such warehouse receipt to the article so manufactured and described in such warehouse receipt, and the Bank shall continue to hold the same and all such right and title, for the same purposes and upon the same conditions as those upon which it previously held such material. 43 V., c. 22, s. 7. (*Substituted for 34 V., c. 5, s. 48.*)

49. All advances made on the security of any bill of lading or warehouse receipt, shall give and be held to give to the Bank making such advances a claim for the repayment of such advances on the goods, wares or merchandize therein mentioned, or into which they have been converted, prior to and by preference over the claim of any unpaid vendor, any law, usage or custom to the contrary notwithstanding. 43 V., c. 22, s. 7. (*Substituted for* 34 V., c. 5, s. 49.) Prior claim of the bank over unpaid vendor.

50. No sale without the consent in writing of the owner, of any timber, boards, deals, staves, saw-logs or other lumber, shall be made under this Act until, nor unless, notice of the time and place of such sale shall have been given by a registered letter, mailed in the post office to the last known address of the pledger thereof, at least thirty days prior to the sale thereof; and no goods, wares or merchandize, other than timber,boards, deals, staves, saw-logs or other lumber, shall be sold by the Bank under this Act without the consent of the owner, until, or unless, notice of the time and place of sale has been given by a registered letter, mailed in the post office to the last known address of the pledger thereof, at least ten days prior to the sale thereof ; and every such sale of any article mentioned in this section, without the consent of the owner, shall be made by public auction after a notice thereof by advertisement, stating the time and place thereof, in at least two newspapers published in or nearest to the place where the sale is to be made ; and if such sale be in the Province of Quebec, then at least one of such newspapers shall be a newspaper published in the English language, and one other such newspaper shall be a newspaper published in the French language. *43 V., c. 22, s. 7. (*Substituted for* 34 V., c. 5, s. 50.) Notice to be given before sale of goods pledged as aforesaid.

51. The Bank shall not make loans or grant discounts on the security of its own stock, but shall have a privileged lien for any debt or liability for any debt to the Bank, on the shares and unpaid dividends of the debtor or party so liable, and may decline to allow any transfer of the shares of such debtor or party until such debt is paid, and if such debt is not paid when due the Bank may sell such shares, after notice has been given to the holder thereof, of the intention of the Bank to sell the same, by mailing such notice in the post office to the last known address of such holder, at least thirty days prior to such sale ; and upon such sale being made, the President, Vice-President, Manager or Cashier shall execute a transfer of such shares to the purchaser thereof in the usual transfer book of the Bank, which transfer shall vest in such purchaser all the rights in or to such shares which were possessed by the holder thereof, with the same obligation of warranty on his part as if he were the vendor thereof, but without any warranty from the Bank or by the officer of the Bank executing such transfer : Lien of bank on stock for overdue debts.

Provision as to collateral security. And nothing in this Act contained shall prevent the Bank from acquiring and holding as collateral security for any advance by or debt to the Bank, or for any credit or liability incurred by the Bank to or on behalf of any person (and either at the time of such advance by, or the contracting of such debt to the Bank, or the opening of such credit, or the incurring of such liability, by the Bank), Dominion, Provincial, British, or Foreign public securities, or the stock, bonds, or debentures of Municipal or other Corporations except Banks; and such stock, bonds, debentures, or securities, may, in case of default to pay the debt for securing which they were so acquired and held, be dealt with, sold and conveyed, in like manner and subject to the same restrictions as are herein provided in respect of stock of the Bank on which it has acquired a lien under this Act; this **Provision may be varied.** provision may, however, be departed from or varied by any agreement between the Bank and the owner of such stock, bonds, debentures or securities, made at the time at which such debt was incurred, or if the time of payment of such debt has been extended, then by an agreement made at the time of such extension. 43 V., c. 22, s. 8. (*Substituted for* 34 V., c. 5, s. 51.)

No penalty for usury. **52.** The Bank shall not be liable to incur any penalty or forfeiture for usury; and may stipulate for, take, reserve or exact any rate of interest or discount not exceeding seven per centum per annum, and may receive and take in advance any such rate, but no higher rate of interest shall be recoverable by the Bank; any rate of interest whatever may be allowed by the Bank upon money deposited with it. 34 V., c. 5, s. 52.

Recital. *2. And whereas in some of the Provinces of Canada, laws may be in force imposing penalties on parties other than Banks, for taking, or stipulating, or paying more than a certain rate of interest, and doubts may arise as to the effect of such laws in certain cases, as to parties other than the Bank, to negotiable securities discounted, or otherwise acquired and **No instrument to be void on ground of usury.** held by any Bank,—therefore it is declared and enacted, that no promissory note, bill of exchange or other negotiable security discounted by, or indorsed or otherwise assigned to any Bank to which this section applies, shall be held to be void, usurious, or tainted by usury, as regards such Bank or any maker, drawer, acceptor, indorser, or indorsee thereof, or other party thereto, or *bonâ fide* holder thereof, nor shall any party thereto be subject to any penalty or forfeiture, by reason of any rate of interest taken, stipulated or received by such Bank, on or with respect to such promissory note, bill of exchange, or other negotiable security, or paid or allowed by any party thereto to another in

---

* This applies only to the Provinces of Ontario, Quebec, Nova Scotia and New Brunswick,

compensation for, or in consideration of the rate of interest taken or to be taken thereon by such Bank,—but no party thereto, other than the Bank, shall be entitled to recover or liable to pay more than the lawful rate of interest in the Province where the suit is brought, nor shall the Bank be entitled to recover a higher rate than seven per cent. per annum; and no innocent holder of or party to any promissory note, bill of exchange, or other negotiable security, shall in any case be deprived of any remedy against any party thereto, or liable to any penalty or forfeiture, by reason of any usury or offence against the laws of any such Province respecting interest, committed in respect of such note, bill or negotiable security, without the complicity or consent of such innocent holder or party. 35 V., c. 8, s 2.

As to innocent holder.

53. The Bank may, in discounting at any of its places of business, branches, agencies or offices of discount and deposit, any note, bill, or other negotiable security or paper payable at any other of its own places or seats of business, branches, agencies or offices of discount and deposit in Canada, receive or retain in addition to the discount, any amount not exceeding the following rates per centum, according to the time it has to run, on the amount of such note, bill or other negotiable security or paper, to defray the expenses attending the collection thereof; that is to say : under thirty days, one-eighth of one per cent.—thirty days or over, but under sixty days, one-fourth of one per cent. —sixty days and over, but under ninety days, three-eighths of one per cent.—ninety days and over, one-half of one per cent. 34 V., c. 5, s. 53.

Collection fees.

54. The Bank may, in discounting any note, bill or other negotiable security or paper, *bond fide* payable at any place in Canada different from that at which it is discounted, and other than one of its own places or seats of business. branches, agencies or offices of discount and deposit in Canada, receive and retain in addition to the discount thereon, a sum not exceeding one-half of one per centum on the amount thereof, to defray the expenses of agency and charges in collecting the same. 34 V., c. 5, s. 54.

Agency fees.

***54** a.* It shall be lawful for any Bank to which this Act applies, (including the Bank of British North America, and La Banque du Peuple) to receive deposits from any person or persons, whomsoever, whatever be his, her, or their age, status or condition in life, and whether such person or persons be qualified by law to enter into ordinary contracts or not; and from time to time to repay any or all of the principal thereof, and to pay the whole or any part of the interest thereon, to such person or persons respectively, without the authority, aid, assistance, or intervention of any per-

Deposits may be received from persons unable to contract.

* This section applies only to the Provinces of Ontario, Quebec, Nova Scotia and New Brunswick.

son or persons, official or officials, being required, unless before such repayment the money so deposited in and repaid by the Bank, be lawfully claimed as the property of some other party, in which case it may be paid to the depositor with the consent of the claimant, or to the claimant with the consent of the depositor, any law, usage, or custom to the

Proviso: amount limited. contrary notwithstanding:—Provided always, that if the person making any deposit, as aforesaid, could not, under the law of the Province where the deposit is made, deposit and withdraw money in and from a Bank without this section, then and in that case the total amount of deposits to be received from such person on deposit shall not at any time exceed the sum of five hundred dollars.

Bank not bound to see to trusts in relation to such deposits. 2. No such Bank shall be bound to see to the execution of any trust whether expressed, implied, or constructive, to which any deposit made under the authority of this section may be subject ; and, except only in the case of lawful claim by some other party before repayment, the receipt of the person in whose name any such deposit stands, or, if it stand in the name of two persons the receipt of one, and if in the names of more than two persons the receipt of a majority of such persons, shall be a sufficient discharge to all concerned for the payment of any money payable in respect of such deposit, notwithstanding any trust to which such deposit may then be subject, and whether or not the Bank sought to be charged with such trust (and with whom the deposit may have been made), had notice thereof ; and no such Bank shall be bound to see to the application of the money paid upon such receipt, any law or usage to the contrary notwithstanding. 35 V., c. 8, ss. 3 *and* 4.

Non-juridical days. 34 *b*. In all matters relating to bills of exchange and promissory notes, the following and no other shall be observed as legal holidays. or non-juridical days, that is to say :—
1. In the Provinces of Ontario, New Brunswick and Nova Scotia,—
Sundays.
New Year's Day.
Good Friday.
Christmas Day.
The birthday (or the day fixed by Proclamation for the celebration of the Birthday) of the reigning Sovereign.
*The first day of July, Dominion Day, and if that day is a Sunday, then the second day of July, under the same name.
Any day appointed by Proclamation for a public holiday or for a general fast, or a general thanksgiving throughout the Dominion ; and the day next following New Year's Day and Christmas Day, when these days respectively fall on Sunday.
And in the Province of Quebec the same days shall be observed as legal holidays, with the addition of,—

---

* Dominion Day is a non-juridical day throughout the Dominion, under 42 V., c. 47.

The Epiphany
The Annunciation.
The Ascension.
Corpus Christi.
St. Peter and St. Paul's Day.
All Saint's Day,
Conception Day.

2. And in any one of the said Provinces of the Dominion any day appointed by Proclamation of the Lieutenant-Governor of such Province for a public holiday or for a fast or thanksgiving within the same

3. And with regard to bills of exchange and promissory notes, whenever the last day of grace falls on a legal holiday or non-juridical day in the Province where any such bill or note is payable, then the day next following not being a legal holiday or non-juridical day in such Province shall be the last day of grace as to such bill or note. 35 V., c. 8, s. 8, *and* 42 V. c. 47.

Bank Notes, Bonds, &c.

55. The bonds, obligations and bills obligatory or of credit of the Bank under its corporate seal and signed by the President or Vice-President and countersigned by a Cashier, or Assistant Cashier, which shall be made payable to any person or persons, shall be assignable by endorsement thereon : and bills or notes of the Bank signed by the President, Vice-President, Cashier or other officer appointed by the Directors of the Bank to sign the same, promising the payment of money to any person or persons, his, her, or their order, or to the bearer, though not under the corporate seal of the Bank, shall be binding and obligatory on it in like manner and with the like force and effect as they would be upon any private person, if issued by him in his private or natural capacity, and shall be assignable in like manner as if they were so issued by a private person in his natural capacity ; Provided always, that nothing in this Act shall be held to debar the Directors of the Bank from authorizing or deputing from time to time any Cashier, Assistant-Cashier or officer of the Bank, or any Director other than the President or Vice-President, or any Cashier, Manager or Local Director of any branch or office of discount and deposit of the Bank, to sign the bills of the Bank intended for general circulation, and payable to order or to bearer on demand. 34 V., c. 5, s. 55. *(marginal: Bonds, notes, &c., how and by whom to be signed. Proviso.)*

56. All Bank notes and bills of the Bank whereon the name or names of any person or persons entrusted or authorized to sign such notes or bills on behalf of the Bank, shall or may become impressed by machinery provided for that purpose by or with the authority of the Bank, shall be and shall be taken to be good and valid to all intents and purposes, as if such notes and bills had been subscribed in the proper handwriting of the person or persons entrusted or authorized by the Bank to sign the same respectively, and *(marginal: Notes may be signed by machinery.)*

shall be and be deemed and taken to be Bank notes and bills within the meaning of all laws and statutes whatever, and shall and may be described as Bank bills or notes in all indictments and civil or criminal proceedings whatsoever, any law, statute or usage to the contrary notwithstanding. 34 V., c. 5, s. 56.

And see s. 78 as to preferential payment of notes of the Bank after 1st July, 1881. in case of insolvency.

INSOLVENCY.

Suspension for 90 days to constitute insolvency.

57. Any suspension by the Bank of payment of any of its liabilities as they accrue, in specie or Dominion notes, shall, if it continues for ninety days, constitute the Bank insolvent and operate a forfeiture of its Charter, so far as regards the issue or reissue of notes and other Banking operations : and the Charter shall remain in force only for the purpose of enabling the Directors or the assignee or assignees, or other legal authority (if any be appointed in such manner as may by law be provided) to make the calls mentioned in the next following section of this Act and to wind up its business : And any such assignee or assignees or other legal authority shall, for such purposes, have all the powers of the Directors. 34 V., c. 5, s. 57.

Liability of shareholders in case of insufficiency of assets.

Calls in such case.

Proviso : as to directors.

58. In the event of the property and assets of the Bank becoming insufficient to pay its debts and liabilities, the shareholders of the Bank shall be liable for the deficiency so far as that each shareholder shall be so liable to an amount (over and above any amount not paid up on their respective shares) equal to the amount of their shares respectively ; and if any suspension of payment in full in specie or Dominion notes, of all or any of the notes or other liabilities of the Bank shall continue for six months, the Directors may and shall make calls on such shareholders, to the amount they may deem necessary to pay all the debts and liabilities of the Bank, without waiting for the collection of any debts due to it or the sale of any of its assets or property ; such calls shall be made at intervals of thirty days and upon notice to be given thirty days at least prior to the day on which such call shall be payable ; and any such call shall not exceed twenty per cent. on each share, and payment thereof may be enforced in like manner as for calls on unpaid stock, and the first of such calls shall be made within ten days after the expiration of the said six months ; and any failure on the part of any shareholder liable to such call to pay the same when due shall operate a forfeiture by such shareholder of all claim in or to any part of the assets of the Bank, such call and any further call thereafter being nevertheless recoverable from him as if no such forfeiture had been incurred. Provided always, that nothing in this section contained shall be construed to alter or diminish the additional liabilities of the Directors hereinbefore mentioned and declared: Provided also, that if the Bank be *en comman- dite* and the principal partners are personally liable, then, in case of any such suspension, such liability shall at once accrue and may be enforced against such principal partners, without waiting for any sale or discussion of the property or assets of the Bank, or other preliminary proceedings whatever, and the provision respecting calls shall not apply to such Bank. 34 V., c. 5, s. 58. *Proviso: as to banks en commandite.*

59. Persons, who having been shareholders in the Bank, have only transferred their shares or any of them to others or registered the transfer thereof within one month before the commencement of the suspension of payment by the Bank. shall be liable to calls on such shares under the next preceding section, as if they had not transferred them, saving their recourse against those to whom they were transferred; and any assignee or other officer or person appointed to wind up the affairs of the Bank, in case of its insolvency, shall have the powers of the Directors with respect to such calls. Provided that if the Bank be *en commandite*, the liability of the principal partners and of the *commanditaires* shall continue for such time after their ceasing to be such as may be provided in the Charter of the Bank, and the foregoing provisions with respect to the transfer of shares or calls shall not apply to such Bank. 34 V., c. 5, s. 59. *Liability of shareholders who have transferred their stock.*

OFFENCES AND PENALTIES.

60. If any Cashier, Assistant Cashier, Manager, Clerk or servant of the Bank secretes, embezzles or absconds with any bond, obligation, bill obligatory or of credit or other bill or note, or any security for money, or any money or effects entrusted to him as such Cashier, Assistant Cashier, Manager, Clerk or Servant, whether the same belong to the said Bank or belong to any person or persons, body or bodies, politic or corporate, or institution or institutions, and be lodged with the said Bank, the said Cashier, Assistant Cashier, Manager, Clerk or Servant, so offending and being thereof convicted in due form of law, shall be deemed guilty of felony, and shall be punished by imprisonment at hard labour in the penitentiary for any term not less than two years, or by imprisonment in any gaol or place of confinement for any term less than two years, in the discretion of the Court. 34 V., c. 5, s. 60. *Embezzlement of bonds, &c., felony.*

61. If any President, Vice-President, Director, Principal Partner *en commandite*, Manager, Cashier or other officer of the Bank wilfully gives or concurs in giving any creditor of the Bank any fraudulent, undue or unfair preference over other creditors, by giving security to such creditor or by changing the nature of his claim or otherwise howsoever, *Fraudulent preference a misdemeanor*

28

he shall be guilty of misdemeanor, and shall further be responsible for all damages sustained by any party by such preference. 34 V., c. 5, s. 61.

62. The making of any wilfully false or deceptive statement in any account, statement, return, report or other document respecting the affairs of the Bank, shall, unless it amounts to a higher offence, be a misdemeanor, and any and every President, Vice-President, Director, Principal Partner *en commandite*, Auditor, Manager, Cashier, or other officer of the Bank preparing, signing, approving or concurring in such statement, return, report or document, or using the same with intent to deceive or mislead any party, shall be held to have wilfully made such false statement, and shall further be responsible for all damages sustained by such party in consequence thereof. 34 V., c. 5, s. 62.

63. Any Director refusing to make or enforce, or to concur in making or enforcing any call under the fifty-eighth section of this Act, shall be deemed guilty of a misdemeanor and shall be personally responsible for any damages suffered by such default. 34 V., c. 5, s. 63.

64. If any miller, warehouseman, master of a vessel, forwarder, carrier, wharfinger, keeper of a cove, yard, harbour or other place for storing timber, deals, staves, boards or other lumber, curer or packer of pork, or dealer in wool, factor agent or other person, or any clerk or person in his employ, knowingly and wilfully gives to any person any writing purporting to be a receipt for, or an acknowledgment of any cereal grain, timber, deals, staves, boards or other lumber, or other goods, wares, merchandize or property, as having been received in his warehouse, vessel, cove, wharf or other place, or in any such place about which he is employed, or as having been in any other manner received by him or the person in or about whose business he is employed, before the goods or property named in such receipt, acknowledgment or writing have been actually so received by or delivered to him or his employer, with the intent to mislead, deceive, injure or defraud any person or persons whomsoever, although such person or persons may be then to him unknown; or if any person knowingly and wilfully accepts or transmits or uses any such false receipt, acknowledgment or writing, the person giving and the person accepting, transmitting or using such false receipt, acknowledgment or writing, shall severally be guilty of a misdemeanor. 34 V., c. 5, s. 64.

65. The wilfully making any false statement in any such receipt, acknowledgment or certificate as in the forty-sixth section of this Act mentioned, or the wilfully alienating or parting with, or not delivering to the holder or indorsee any cereal grain, goods, wares or merchandize mentioned in such receipt, acknowledgment or certificate, contrary to the undertaking therein expressed or implied, shall be a misdemeanor. 34 V., c. 5, s. 65.

66. If any offence in either of the two next preceding sections mentioned be committed by the doing of anything in the name of any firm, company or copartnership of persons, the person by whom such thing is actually done, and any person who connives at the doing thereof, shall be deemed guilty of the offence, and not any other person. 34 V., c. 5, s. 66.

Offences by members of a partnership.

66a. After the first day of July, one thousand eight hundred and eighty, any person, firm or company assuming or using the title of "Bank" without being authorized so to do by this Act, or by some other Act in force in that behalf, shall be guilty of a misdemeanor. 43 V., c. 22, s. 10.

Unauthorised use of title "Bank," a misdemeanor.

67. Any person convicted of a misdemeanor under this Act shall, on conviction, be liable to be imprisoned in any gaol or place of confinement for any term not exceeding two years, in the discretion of the Court before which the conviction shall be had. 34 V., c. 5, s. 67.

Punishment for misdemeanor.

68. No private person or party, except a chartered Bank, shall issue or re-issue, make, draw, or indorse any bill, bond, note, check or other instrument, intended to circulate as money, or to be used as a substitute for money, for any amount whatever, under a penalty of four hundred dollars, to be recovered with costs, in any court having civil jurisdiction to the amount, by any party who will sue for the same ; and one-half of such sum shall belong to the party suing for the same, and the other half to Her Majesty, for the public uses of the Dominion.

Chartered Banks only to issue notes for circulation.

The intention to pass any such instrument as money, shall be presumed, if it be made for the payment of a less sum than twenty dollars, and be payable either in form or in fact to the bearer thereof, or at sight or on demand, or at less than thirty days thereafter, or be overdue, or be in any way calculated or designed for circulation, or as a substitute for money ; unless such instrument be a check on some chartered Bank, paid by the maker directly to his immediate creditor, or a promissory note, bill of exchange, bond or other undertaking, for the payment of money paid or delivered by the maker thereof to his immediate creditor, and be not designed to circulate as a substitute for money. 34 V., c. 5, s. 68.

What shall be deemed such notes.

How notices shall be given.

69. The several public notices by this Act required to be given, shall be given by advertisement in one or more of the newspapers published at the place where the Head Office of the Bank is situate, and in the *Canada Gazette* or such other *Gazette* as shall be generally known and described as the *Official Gazette* for the publication of official documents and notices emanating from the Civil Government of the Dominion. 34 V., c. 5, s. 69.

FUTURE LEGISLATION.

Bank to be subject to any future winding up Act.

70. The Bank shall be subject to such provisions of any general or special winding up Act to be passed by Parliament as may be declared to apply to Banks; and no special Act which Parliament may deem it right to pass for winding up the affairs of the Bank in case of its insolvency, shall be deemed an infringement of its rights or of the privileges conferred by its charter. 34 V., c. 5, s. 70.

And any general Bank Act.

71. The Bank shall always be subject to any general provisions respecting Banks which Parliament may deem necessary for the public interest. 34 V., c. 5, s. 71.

SPECIAL PROVISIONS AS TO CERTAIN BANKS.

What sections shall apply to Bank of P.N.A.

72. The Bank of British North America, which, by the terms of its present charter, is to be subject to the general laws of the Dominion, with respect to Banks and Banking, shall not issue or re-issue in Canada, any note for a less sum than four dollars, and any such note of the said Bank outstanding shall be called in and redeemed as soon as practicable :* and the provisions contained in the ninth, twelfth, thirteenth, fourteenth, fifteenth, sixteenth, forty-fifth, forty-sixth, forty-seventh, forty-eighth, forty-ninth, fiftieth, fifty-first, fifty-second, fifty-third, fifty-fourth, fifty-fourth (*a*), fifty-fourth (*b*), fifty-sixth, sixtieth, sixty-first, sixty-second, sixty-fourth, sixty-fifth, sixty-sixth, sixty-seventh, sixty-ninth, seventy-first and seventy-eighth sections of this Act, shall apply to the said Bank ; those contained in the other sections shall not apply to it. 34 V., c. 5, s. 72, *as amended by* 35 V., c. 8, 40 V., c. 54, *and* 43 V., c. 22.

How certain Banks may come under this Act.

73. This Act shall not apply to any now existing Bank not mentioned in the schedule B thereunto annexed (except the Bank of British North America to the extent aforesaid and La Banque du Peuple to the extent hereinafter mentioned) unless the Directors of such Bank shall, by special resolution, apply to the Treasury Board, that the provisions

---

* But see s. 78 as to issue of notes after 1st July. 1881.

of this Act may be extended to such Bank, nor unless the Treasury Board allows such application, and upon publication in the *Official Gazette* of such resolution, and of the minute of the Treasury Board thereon, allowing such application, such Bank shall come under the provisions of this Act. 34 V., c. 5, s. 73.

74. In pursuance of the application made by the Bank of Nova Scotia in that behalf, it shall be lawful for the shareholders of the said Bank, at any special general meeting called for the purpose, and by a by-law to be passed thereat, to reduce the capital and shares of the said Bank by an amount not exceeding thirteen per cent. thereof respectively. and the shares and capital shall thereafter be reckoned at the amount to which they shall be so reduced. 34 V., c. 5, s. 74. *Capital of Bank of N.S. may be reduced.*

75. All the provisions of this Act except those contained in sections one, two, three, five, six, seven, twenty-seven, twenty-nine, thirty, thirty-one, thirty-two, thirty-three, thirty-five, thirty-six, thirty-seven, fifty-seven, fifty-eight, fifty-nine, sixty-three, seventy, seventy-two, seventy-three, and seventy-four, and so much of section twenty-eight, as is declared not to apply to the Banks *en commandite* shall apply to La Banque du Peuple : Provided that wherever the word " Directors " is used in any of the sections which apply to the said Bank it shall be read and construed as meaning the principal partners or members of the corporation of the said Bank ; and so much of the Act incorporating the said Bank or of any Act amending or continuing it as may be inconsistent with any section of this Act applying to the said Bank or which makes any provision in any matter provided for by the said sections other than such as is hereby made is hereby repealed. 34 V., c. 5, s. 75. *What provisions shall apply to La Banque du Peuple.* *Proviso.*

REPEALING AND SAVING CLAUSES.

76. The Act passed in the thirty-third year of Her Majesty's reign, chaptered eleven, and intituled, *An Act respecting Banks and Banking*, is hereby repealed, and the Act passed in the thirty-first year of Her Majesty's reign, and intituled, *An Act respecting Banks*, is hereby repealed in so far as respects Banks to which this Act applies, including the Bank of British North America, and La Banque du Peuple, and shall cease to apply to them after the passing of this Act (or after they respectively come under its provisions, if they are now existing Banks and not mentioned in the Schedule B), except as to rights theretofore acquired under or. offences committed against it. 34 V., c. 5, s. 76. *Certain Acts repealed, 33 V., c. 11.* *31 V., c. 11, as to certain Banks.*

2. Sections three, four, five and six of the Act passed in the forty-second year of Her Majesty's reign, chaptered forty-five, and intituled " *An Act to amend the Act relating to* *42 V., c. 45, ss. 3, 4, 5 & 6, as to numbering shares.*

Banks and Banking and the Acts amending the same," and

chapter fifty-five of the Consolidated Statutes of the late Province of Canada, intituled *"An Act respecting Banks and freedom of Banking,"* are hereby repealed, except as to rights acquired, offences committed, or liabilities incurred before the passing of this Act.   43 V , c. 22, s. 9.

Saving pending cases.

77 Nothing in this Act contained shall affect any case pending when it shall come into force, but such case shall be decided as if this Act had not been passed.   34 V.. c. 5, s. 77.

After 1st July, 1881,

78 After the time when the Charters of the said Banks respectively would have expired if they had not been continued by the second sub-section of section one of this Act.—

Notes to be first charge on assets.

(1.) The payment of the notes issued by any such Bank and intended for circulation, then outstanding, shall be the first charge upon the assets of the Bank in case of its insolvency ;

No note under $5 or other than a multiple of $5.

(2.) No Bank note for a sum less than five dollars, or for any sum not being a multiple of five dollars, shall be issued or re-issued by any such Bank, and all notes for a less sum than five dollars, or not being such multiple as aforesaid, heretofore issued shall be called in and cancelled as soon as may be practicable ;

Payments in Dominion Notes.

(3.) Any such Bank when making any payment, shall, on the request of the person to whom the payment is to be made, pay the same, or such part thereof not exceeding fifty dollars as such person may request, in Dominion notes for one or for two dollars each, at the option of the receiver ;

Renewal of proxies.

(4.) No appointment of a proxy to vote at any meeting of the shareholders of the Bank shall be valid for that purpose, unless made or renewed in writing within the three years next preceding the time of such meeting ;

As to Bank of B.N.A.

(5.) The provisions in this section shall, from and after the first day of July, one thousand eight hundred and eighty-one, apply to the Bank of British North America, which by the terms of its present charter is to be subject to the general laws of the Dominion with respect to Banks and Banking.   43 V., c. 22, s. 12.

SCHEDULE A.

An Act respecting the protection of Persons who receive Assignments and enter into Contracts in relation to Goods entrusted to Agents.

HER MAJESTY, by and with the advice and consent of the Legislative Council and Assembly of Canada, enacts as follows :—

1. Any person may contract for the purchase of goods with any agent entrusted with the possession thereof, or to whom the same may be consigned, and may receive and pay for the same to such agent, and such contract and payment shall be binding upon the owner of the goods notwithstanding the purchaser has notice that he is contracting only with an agent. *When contracts with agents to be valid.*

2. Any agent entrusted with the possession of goods or of the documents of title thereto shall be deemed the owner thereof for the following purposes, that is to say : *When agents to be deemed owners.*

1. To make a sale or contract, as in the first clause mentioned ;

2. To entitle the consignee of goods consigned by such agent to a lien thereon for any money or negotiable security advanced or given by him to or for the use of such agent, or received by the agent for the use of the consignee, in like manner as if such agent was the true owner of the goods ;

3. To give validity to any contract or agreement by way of pledge (*gage*) lien or security *bonâ fide* made with such agent, as well for an original loan, advance or payment made upon the security of the goods or documents, as for any further or continuing advance in respect thereof; and

4. To make such contract binding upon the owner of the goods and on all other persons interested therein, notwithstanding the person claiming such pledge or lien had notice that he was contracting only with an agent.

3. In case any person has a valid lien and security on any goods or document of title or negotiable security in respect of a previous advance upon a contract with an agent,—and in case he delivers up the same to such agent upon a contract for the pledge (*gage*), lien or security of other goods or of *What contracts for lien valid.*

3

another document or security by such agent delivered to him in exchange, to be held upon the same lien as the goods, document or security so delivered up,—then such new contract, if *bona fide*, shall be deemed a valid contract made in consideration of a present advance of money within this Act, but the lien acquired under such new contract on the goods, document or security deposited in exchange, shall not exceed the value of the goods, document or security so delivered up and exchanged.

Must be *bona fide*.

4. Such contracts only shall be valid as are herein mentioned, and such loans, advances and exchanges only shall be valid as are made *bona fide* and without notice that the agent making the same has no authority so to do, or that he is acting *mala fide* against the owner of the goods.

Antecedent debt not to authorize lien.

5. No antecedent debt owing from any agent entrusted as aforesaid, shall authorize any lien (*gage*) or pledge in respect of such debt, nor shall it authorize such agent to deviate from any express orders or authority received from his principal.

Bona fide transactions with agents bind owners.

6. All *bona fide* loans, advances and exchanges as aforesaid (though made with notice of the agent not being the owner, but without notice of his acting without authority), shall bind the owner and all other persons interested in the goods, document or security, as the case may be.

Documents of title defined.

7. Every bill of lading, warehouse keeper's or wharfinger's receipt or order for delivery of goods, every bill of inspection of pot or pearl ashes, and every other document used in the ordinary course of business, as proof of the possession or control of goods, or authorizing or purporting to authorize either by endorsement or by delivery, the possessor of such document to transfer or receive goods thereby represented, shall be deemed a document of title within this Act.

Agents possessed of, to be deemed entrusted, &c.

8. Any agent entrusted as aforesaid and possessed of any such document of title, whether derived immediately from the owner of the goods or obtained by reason of the agent having been entrusted with the possession of the goods or of any document of title thereto, shall be deemed to be entrusted with the possession of the goods represented by such document of title.

Contracts for a lien founded thereon valid.

9. All contracts pledging or giving a lien upon any such document of title shall be deemed a pledge (*gage*) of and lien upon the goods to which it relates, and the agent shall be deemed the possessor of the goods or documents of title whether the same be in his actual custody or be held by any other person for him or subject to his control.

10. When any loan or advance is *bonâ fide* made to any **Bonâ fide** agent entrusted with and in possesion of goods or documents **loans or advances** of title as aforesaid on the faith of any contract in writing to **when deemed** consign, deposit, transfer or deliver such goods or documents **authorized.** of title, and the same are actually received by the person making the loan or advance, either at the time of the contract or at a time subsequent thereto, without notice that the agent is not authorized to make the pledge or security, such loan or advance shall be deemed a loan or advance upon the security of the goods or documents of title within this Act.

11. Every contract, whether made direct with the agent **What con-** as aforesaid, or with any clerk or other person on his behalf **tracts to be as considered.** shall be deemed a contract with such agent.

12. Every payment, whether made by money, bills of ex- **Payments,** change or other negotiable security, shall be deemed an **when deemed advances.** advance within this Act.

13. Every agent in possession of goods or documents as **Possession** aforesaid shall, for the purposes of this Act, be taken to be **primâ facie evidence of** entrusted therewith by the owner, unless the contrary be **ownership.** shewn in evidence.

14. Nothing herein contained shall lessen, alter or affect **Other** the civil responsibility of any agent for the breach of any **liability of agents not to** duty or contract or the non-fulfilment of his orders or **be affected.** authority, in respect of any such contract, agreement, lien or pledge (*gage*) as aforesaid.

15. In case any agent entrusted as aforesaid, contrary to or **Consequences** without the authority of his principal, for his own benefit **of dereliction.** and in violation of good faith, makes, by way of pledge (*gage*), lien and security, any consignment, deposit, transfer or delivery of any goods or documents of title so entrusted to him, or contrary to or without such authority, for his own benefit and in violation of good faith, accepts any advance on the faith of any contract to consign, deposit, transfer or deliver such goods or documents of title, such agent shall be deemed guilty of a misdemeanor, and being convicted thereof, **Misdemeanor.** shall be sentenced to suffer such punishment by fine or imprisonment in the common gaol for any term not exceeding two years, or by both, as the Court awards.

16. Every clerk or other person who knowingly and wil- **Aiders, &c.** fully acts and assists in making any such consignment, deposit, transfer or delivery, or in accepting or procuring such advance as aforesaid, shall be guilty of a misdemeanor, and shall be liable, at the discretion of the court, to any of the punishments which the Court may award, as herein last mentioned.

When agent not liable criminally.

17. No such agent shall be liable to any prosecution for consigning, depositing, transferring or delivering any such goods or documents of title, in case the same are not made a security for or subject to the payment of any greater sum of money than at the time was justly due and owing to the agent from his principal, together with the amount of any bills of exchange drawn by or on account of his principal, and accepted by such agent.

Conviction not admissible in evidence.

18. The conviction of any agent as aforesaid shall not be received in evidence in any action at law, or suit in equity against him.

Admissions under oath not admissible in evidence against the party.

19. No oath, or admission under oath, by an agent entrusted as aforesaid, made previously to his being indicted for the offence, in consequence of the compulsory process of a Court of Law, Equity or Admiralty in an action, suit or proceeding *bond fide* instituted by a party aggrieved, nor any disclosure made by him in an examination or in a deposition before any Commissioner of Bankrupts, shall be used in evidence in any prosecution against the agent in respect of any act done by him as aforesaid.

Owners may redeem goods pledged.

20. Nothing herein contained shall prevent the owner from redeeming any goods or documents of title pledged as aforesaid, at any time before the same have been sold, upon repayment of the amount of the lien thereon or restoration of the securities in respect of which the lien exists, and upon payment or satisfaction to the agent of any sum of money for or in respect of which such agent is entitled to retain the goods or documents, by way of lien against such owner ; or shall prevent the owner from recovering from the person with whom any goods or documents have been pledged, or who has any lien thereon, any balance or sum of money remaining in his hands as the produce of the sale of the goods, after deducting the amount of the lien under the contract.

Remedy of owner against the estate of an agent bankrupt.

21. In case of the bankruptcy of any such agent, and in case the owner of the goods redeems the same, he shall, in respect of the sum paid by him on account of the agent for such redemption, be held to have paid the same for the use of such agent before his bankruptcy, or in case the goods have not been so redeemed, the owner shall be deemed a creditor of the agent for the value of the goods so pledged at the time of the pledge, and may in either case prove for or set-off the sum so paid, or the value of such goods, as the case may be.

Interpretation clause.

22. In construing this Act, the word "person" shall be taken to designate a body corporate or company as well as an individual ; and the word "goods" shall be taken to

include all personal property of whatever nature or kind
soever, and the word " shipped " shall be taken to mean the
carriage of goods, whether by land or by water.

23. Nothing herein contained shall give validity to, or in This Act not
any wise affect any contract, agreement, lien, pledge (*gage*), to affect
or other act, matter, or thing made or done before the twenty- prior to 28th
eighth of July, 1847, or destroy or diminish any other right, July, 1847.
recourse or remedy not contrary or repugnant to this Act
which might be enforced according to the Laws of Upper or
Lower Canada.

24. This Act shall relate to and from the twenty-eighth Act to relate
July, one thousand eight hundred and forty-seven, and as to 28th July,
respects all transactions and things since that day within 1847.
the scope and meaning hereof, shall be construed and applied as if it had been passed on that day. 43 V., c. 22,
Schedule A.

SCHEDULE B.

BANKS WHOSE CHARTERS ARE CONTINUED BY THIS ACT.

1. The Bank of Montreal.
2. The Quebec Bank.
3. La Banque du Peuple.
4. The Consolidated Bank.
5. Molson's Bank.
6. The Bank of Toronto.
7. The Ontario Bank.
8. The Eastern Townships Bank.
9. La Banque Nationale.
10. La Banque Jacques Cartier.
11. The Merchants' Bank of Canada.
12. The Union Bank of Lower Canada.
13. The Canadian Bank of Commerce.
14. The Mechanics' Bank.
15. The Dominion Bank.
16. The Merchants' Bank of Halifax.
17. The Bank of Nova Scotia.
18. The Bank of Yarmouth.
19. The Bank of Liverpool.
20. The Exchange Bank of Canada.
21. La Banque Ville Marie.
22. The Standard Bank of Canada.
23. The Bank of Hamilton.
24. The Halifax Banking Company.
25. The Maritime Bank of the Dominion of Canada.
26. The Federal Bank of Canada.
27. La Banque d'Hochelaga.

28. The Stadacona Bank.
29. The Imperial Bank of Canada.
30. The Pictou Bank.
31. La Banque de St. Hyacinthe.
32. The Bank of Ottawa.
33. The Bank of New Brunswick.
34. The Exchange Bank of Yarmouth.
35. The Union Bank of Halifax.
36. The People's Bank of Halifax.—43 V., c. 22, *Schedule B.*

43 VICTORIA.

CHAP. 13.

An Act further to amend the Acts respecting Dominion Notes.

[Assented to 7th May, 1880.]

Preamble.

WHEREAS it is expedient to make further provision respecting the issue of Dominion Notes: Therefore Her Majesty, by and with the advice and consent of the Senate and House of Commons of Canada, enacts as follows :—

Act 38 V., c. 5 and others limiting amount of Dominion Notes repealed, and amount limited to $20,000,000.

1. So much of the Act passed in the thirty-eighth year of Her Majesty's reign, intituled "*An Act further to amend the Acts regulating the issue of Dominion Notes,*" or of any other Act now in force, as limits the amount of Dominion Notes to be issued and outstanding at any time to twelve million dollars, or as fixes the amount to be held in specie for the redemption of any such notes, is hereby repealed, and the amount of Dominion Notes issued and outstanding at any time may, by Order in Council, founded on a report of the Treasury Board, be increased to but shall not exceed twenty million dollars, by amounts not exceeding one million dollars at one time, and not exceeding four million dollars in any one year:

Proviso: amount in gold and guaranteed Dominion securities to be held for redemption. And in unguaranteed Dominion debentures.

Provided that the Minister of Finance shall always hold, for securing the redemption of such notes issued and outstanding, an amount in gold, or in gold and Dominion securities guaranteed by the Government of the United Kingdom, equal to not less than twenty-five per cent. of the amount of such notes,—at least fifteen per cent. of the total amount of such notes being so held in gold; and provided also that the said Minister shall always hold for the redemption of such notes an amount equal to the remaining seventy-five per cent. of the total amount thereof, in Dominion debentures issued by authority of Parliament.

2. Debentures of the Dominion may be issued and delivered to the Minister of Finance, for the general purposes of this Act, and to enable him to comply with its requirements, such debentures being held as aforesaid for securing the redemption of Dominion Notes, and the said Minister having full power to dispose of them, and of the guaranteed debentures aforesaid, either temporarily or absolutely, in order to raise funds for such redemption, and for the purpose of procuring the amounts of gold required to be held by him under this Act; but nothing herein contained shall be construed to authorize the issue of debentures not otherwise authorized by Parliament, or any increase of the debt of the Dominion beyond the amount so authorized.

Debentures may be delivered to Minister of Finance, and disposed of by him for the purposes of this Act.

Proviso.

3. The Minister of Finance shall publish monthly in the *Canada Gazette* a statement of the amount of Dominion Notes outstanding on the last day of the preceding month, and of the gold, guaranteed debentures and unguaranteed debentures then held by him for securing the redemption thereof, distinguishing the amounts of each so held at each of the cities at which Dominion Notes are redeemable; such statements being made up from returns to be made by the branch offices, bank or banks, at which such notes are redeemable, to the said Minister.

Minister of Finance to publish monthly statements under this Act.

4. The Governor may, in his discretion, establish branch offices of the Receiver General's Department at Winnipeg, Charlottetown and Victoria, respectively, or any of them, for the redemption of Dominion Notes, or may make arrangements with any chartered bank or banks for the redemption thereof at the said cities, in like manner as he may now do at the cities of Montreal, Toronto, Halifax and St. John (N.B.) and under like provisions: Provided that any Assistant Receiver General appointed at any of the said cities under the Act of the thirty-fourth Victoria, chapter six, shall be an agent for the issue and redemption of such notes.

Offices of redemption at certain cities.

Proviso: under 34 V., c. 6, s. 19.

5. So much of the hitherto unrepealed portions of the Act passed in the thirty-first year of Her Majesty's reign, chaptered forty-six, and intituled *"An Act to enable Banks in any part of Canada to use notes of the Dominion instead of issuing notes of their own,"* or of the Act passed in the thirty-third year of Her Majesty's reign, and intituled *"An Act to amend the Act 31 Victoria, chapter 46, and to regulate the issue of Dominion Notes,"* as is inconsistent with the provisions of this Act or makes any provision in any matter provided for by this Act, is hereby repealed; but the provisions of the said Acts not hitherto repealed and not inconsistent with this Act shall remain in force and apply to Dominion Notes issued or re-issued under the authority thereof or of this Act; and such notes shall be a legal

Repeal of inconsistent enactments now in force. 31 V., c. 46.

33 V., c. 10.

Provisions not inconsistent with this Act to apply.

tender in every part of the Dominion except at the offices at which they are respectively made payable ; the proceeds thereof shall form part of the Consolidated Revenue Fund of Canada, and the expenses lawfully incurred under the said Acts or this Act shall be paid out of the said fund.

INDEX.

www.ingramcontent.com/pod-product-compl ance
Lightning Source LLC
Chambersburg PA
CBHW021600270326
41931CB00009B/1309